Specialising in lyrical non-fictio... ...NG
and **BRITA** ... **RANSTRÖM** have ... ...ped their unique approach

over 15 years ...aring the illustration between them and mixing words
and pictures ...ll sorts of inventive and delightful ways, they have won
many ...ds including the Nestlé/Smarties Silver Award,
and are ... times winners of The English Association Award.
Mick Man... ...l in love with wildlife on primary school nature walks
45 yea... ...and has an MA in natural history illustration from
the Roy... ...ege of Art. Brita Granström grew up on a farm and
she has a... ...from Konstfack in Stockholm. They are married with
4 childrer... ...l spend their time between England and a small red
house in ...eden – which they designed and built themselves.
Their ... ks with Frances Lincoln include: *Tail-End Charlie*,
Taff in the ...AF (winner of the English Association Award 2011),
What I ...Darwin Saw, *Charles Dickens: an extraordinary life*,
Woolly Ma...th, *Dino Dinners* and the award winning Fly on the Wall
series (*R...Fort*, *Viking Longship*, *Pharaoh's Egypt* and *Greek Hero*).

...out more about Mick and Brita's books at:
www.mickandbrita.com.

This book is dedicated to The Wildlife Trusts,
working hard to conserve the full range
of the UK's habitats and species – *Mick and Brita*

The authors and publisher would like to thank
David North and The Wildlife Trusts
for their help with this book

JANETTA OTTER-BARRY BOOKS

First published in Great Britain and in the USA in 2011 by
Frances Lincoln Children's Books,
4 Torriano Mews, Torriano Avenue,
London NW5 2RZ
www.franceslincoln.com

First paperback edition published in Great Britain in 2012

A catalogue record for this book is available from the British Library

ISBN 978-1-84780-326-9

The illustrations in this book are in pencil and watercolour.
Mick has done most of the natural history drawings while Brita has drawn the people,
a selection of the plants, some seaside creatures and the hand lettering.
Find out more about Mick and Brita's books at: www.mickandbrita.com.

Set in Rockwell

Printed in Dongguan, Guangdong, China by Toppan Leefung in December 2011
The interiors of this book are made from 100% virgin pulp from a sustainable forest.

1 3 5 7 9 8 6 4 2

NATURE
ADVENTURES

Mick Manning & Brita Granström

F

FRANCES LINCOLN
CHILDREN'S BOOKS

CONTENTS

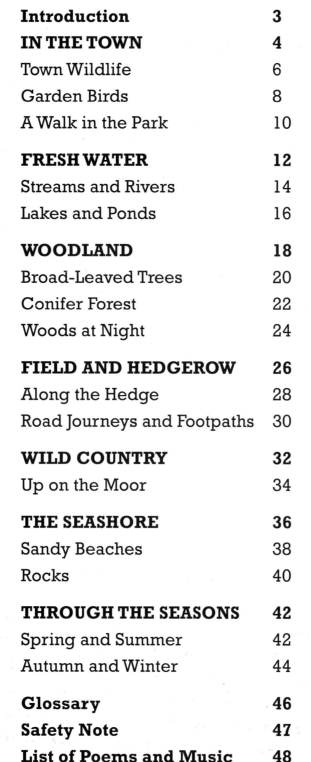

INTRODUCTION

Your family doesn't need to be hiking through dramatic wilderness to have a nature adventure. A nature adventure can happen anywhere, any time – wherever you are. Even a wander down the high street can be exciting once you learn how to look and listen. This little book is squeezed full of our favourite nature adventures. It will help you to watch wildlife and identify sounds, tracks and signs. The nature 'adventurers' we have drawn in the book also quote snatches of poetry, because we don't think of nature as just a science subject – it's a treasure trove! We hope our book will inspire you to draw, write and read about nature too. . . and to have nature adventures of your own.
'Long live the weeds and the wilderness yet.'

Useful Things

Binoculars and a **hand lens** or **magnifying glass** are very useful for nature adventures. **Warm clothes**, **waterproof shoes** and a **rainproof coat** are pretty important too.

A **rucksack** is a good way to carry round a **notebook** and **pencil** and maybe a **picnic** with a **warm flask** or a **bottle of water**. A pair of **disposable gloves** and some **plastic bags** for nature finds are a good idea. A **mobile phone** is a sensible precaution, and last but not least **an adult** can be very useful and help out with all sorts of things.

IN THE TOWN

Early signs of spring:

Daffodil

Snowdrop

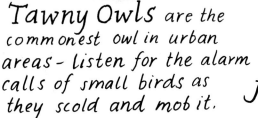

Tawny Owls are the commonest owl in urban areas - listen for the alarm calls of small birds as they scold and mob it.

Jackdaws say 'Jack!'

Rooks often choose churchyards for their communal rookeries. Rooks say 'Caw!'

In the Town

Some of the easiest places to have nature adventures and get close to wildlife can be in built-up areas, because urban wild creatures get used to seeing humans. Begin by checking out the area you live in: birds through your window, squirrels and pigeons in the park. Take a ramble through a cemetery or visit a reservoir. Start a notebook and write down what you see and when and where. Get to know your local 'patch' in different seasons and you'll be surprised at what turns up.

Pineapple weed loves waste-ground. Smells fruity when crushed.

Pipistrelle Bat

Long-Eared Bat

Bats leave crumbly droppings and insect remains where they feed and roost.

Look out for **urban foxes** and their musky scent.

Tracks

House Mice live in buildings and sheds.

5

Town Wildlife

The wildlife in a town can be amazing when you look closely. It's a place to look again at things we sometimes take for granted: a singing starling, the amazing colour of sycamore buds, the egg-yolk-yellow of dandelions or a nettle patch heaving with hairy caterpillars. Try a simple plant and mini-beast survey, by pegging out a 1 metre by 1 metre (3 feet by 3 feet) square using sticks and string. The variety of animals and plants you find within your chosen area is known as 'species diversity'. Using your notebook, list what you see, then try your surveying skills in a larger 'enclosed' habitat such as a garden, churchyard or park.

Woodlice are common in the garden.

Orb Spiders build beautiful webs to catch their prey.

Sycamore buds

Zebra Spiders stalk and jump on their prey.

Ivy provides good cover for nesting birds.

'I know a bank where the wild thyme blows.'
William Shakespeare

Cool!

Many birds and animals eat worms, beetle grubs, slugs and snails.

Cockchafer Beetle Grub

Dock leaf - dulls the pain of nettle stings

Blackbird

female   male

Earthworm

Gently pour a bucket of water over your survey area to bring worms to the surface.

Slug

Hedgehogs hunt at night. Look out for black tarry droppings on lawns.

Snail

Centipede

Millipede

Earwig

Ladybird

Male 'pussy willow' catkins of the Goat Willow or Sallow

Four common garden insects:

Wasp   Bumblebee   Bluebottle   Hoverfly

Butterflies love park and garden flowers.

Cabbage White and caterpillar

Peacock

Red Admiral

Tortoiseshell

Look for caterpillars on plants like Nettle and Cabbage.

Buddleia

Peacock Caterpillars' dark skin soaks up the sun.

Hatching pupae

Rosebay Willow Herb loves waste ground and railway embankments.

Nettles Ouch!

White Dead-Nettles do not sting.

Dandelion

'clock' or seedhead

Daisy

7

Grey Squirrels are clever acrobats, but carry a disease called Squirrel Pox, fatal to Red Squirrels.

Garden Birds

Together, gardens make up the largest area of town green space. Animals rely on them as places to shelter, find food and rear their young. Providing food, water and nest boxes will bring wildlife closer to you. Plants that attract butterflies and bees are a great idea too. Even a window box can become a tiny nature reserve. Always avoid using pesticides because 'pests' are food for many other living things, and poisons can pass along the food chain. For example, slug to hedgehog or snail to thrush.

Blue Tit

Coal Tit

Great Tit

Hanging peanuts will attract tits and finches.

Garden birds need water too.

Bullfinch male

Starling male

House Sparrow

Tree Sparrow

Greenfinch

Chaffinch male

Goldfinch male

Bird tables will attract local birds to your garden or window.

Peanuts, seeds and table scraps (such as bacon rind, wholemeal breadcrumbs, cooked rice, etc) will be popular... but tidy up or you will also attract rats!

Brown Rats carry diseases and germs.

"I hope we get blue tits nesting in here!"

Hang nest boxes to attract garden birds.

The Mistle Thrush will chase away egg thieves like Magpies.

The Mistle Thrush will sing through a storm – 'The Stormcock'.

A Song Thrush's egg and nest

Song Thrush's 'anvil' – used to break snail shells.

Swallow: liquid jumble of twitters and clicks

Starling: helter-skelter whistles and mimicry from car alarms to curlews

Song Thrush: delicious song, often repeats itself

In late spring, get up early and listen to the 'dawn chorus'!

Blackbird: rich, melodic whistling song

Dunnock: a rambling ditty

Robin: 'liquid' trills by day and night

Blue Tit: "tsee-tsee tsee-see-see!"

Wren: twittering song-bursts. Loud for its size.

Great Tit (on Common Lime): "Seee-saw, seee-saw"

9

Rowan berries attract many hungry birds.

Rowan Tree

Common Pigeons

Town Pigeon
Bubbly "crooo-cooo!"

Herring Gulls are common urban scavengers.

Squabbling

juvenile plumage   winter plumage

Wood Pigeons seem to croon: "It's hur-ting mummmmy It's hur-ting mummmmy."

winter   summer

Collared Dove
"Kooo-coo-koo!"

Black-Headed Gulls actually have a brown head.

Moorhens and Coots are common, even in parks.

Mute Swans are beautiful, but can be aggressive when defending nests or cygnets.

'And the ducks all quacked as if they were daft And it sounded as if the old drake laughed.'

Coots are easily recognise by their white beak shield.

Mallard

female   mal

Park ponds are a good place to see water-birds close up...

male   female

Tufted Duck

10

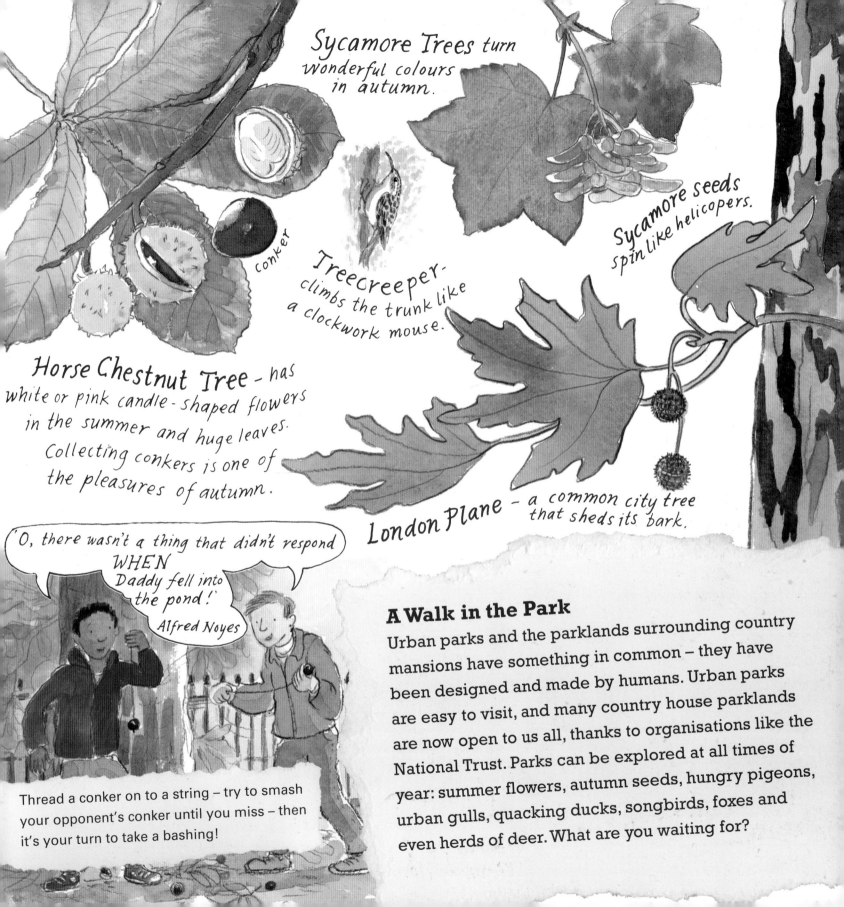

Sycamore Trees turn wonderful colours in autumn.

conker

Treecreeper - climbs the trunk like a clockwork mouse.

Sycamore seeds spin like helicopers.

Horse Chestnut Tree - has white or pink candle - shaped flowers in the summer and huge leaves. Collecting conkers is one of the pleasures of autumn.

London Plane - a common city tree that sheds its bark.

'O, there wasn't a thing that didn't respond WHEN Daddy fell into the pond!'
Alfred Noyes

Thread a conker on to a string – try to smash your opponent's conker until you miss – then it's your turn to take a bashing!

A Walk in the Park

Urban parks and the parklands surrounding country mansions have something in common – they have been designed and made by humans. Urban parks are easy to visit, and many country house parklands are now open to us all, thanks to organisations like the National Trust. Parks can be explored at all times of year: summer flowers, autumn seeds, hungry pigeons, urban gulls, quacking ducks, songbirds, foxes and even herds of deer. What are you waiting for?

FRESH WATER

'All along the backwater,
Through the rushes tall,'

'Ducks are a-dabbling,
Up tails all!'

Ratty sings that in
The Wind in the Willows.

male Teal

The Dabchick dives for small fish and insects.

chick

male Pintail

Great Crested Grebes also dive for fish.

Goldeneye are diving ducks and winter visitors.

Black-Throated Diver

Wigeon gather in huge flocks in winter.

female

male

male

Divers are rare birds with a haunting call. They nest in wild places like the Scottish highlands.

Red-Throated Diver

female

Look for the velvety sausage-shaped seed heads of the Bulrush.

Fresh Water

These habitats include lakes and rivers as well as 'man-made' reservoirs and canals. But don't forget rushing streams, drainage ditches, park lakes - even tiny garden ponds. All sorts of animals live in and around fresh water, and many others visit it to drink, bathe and hunt for food. What you might see depends on where you are; so although many animals on these pages, such as ducks, dragonflies and pike, are common in different habitats, you'll only see black or red-throated divers breeding in the far north - although they do turn up around the coast during the winter.

Common Reeds grow in dense reed beds.

Dragonflies spend up to four years as fierce underwater nymphs...

Nymph

...after that they crawl out to become dragonflies.

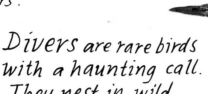
Emperor Dragonfly

Pond Skaters can walk on water.

Water Boatmen swim with hairy back legs.

Streams and Rivers

From tiny beginnings, small streams splash, gurgle and join together to become rivers that flow into estuaries and finally the sea. Fish such as salmon and sea trout swim up them to spawn and otters, herons, kingfishers and voles live there. They know that the bed of any healthy river or stream is full of insects, fish and water plants, and its muddy banks, especially around the estuary, contain worms, snails and shellfish. Of course many of these animals live in lakes and ponds as well, so keep your eyes open.

'Oh let them be left, wildness and wet;'

'Long live the weeds and the wilderness yet.' wrote Gerard Manley Hopkins.

A flying Kingfisher is a living jewel.

Otter droppings have a sweet, musky scent.

Mink droppings stink!

If you see an **Otter**, wait until it dives before creeping closer.

The **Kingfisher** dives from its perch to catch small fish.

otter track

Pied Wagtail

Mink are escapees from fur farms. They are good swimmers and eat anything they can find.

Indian Balsam or 'Jumping Jack' seedpods 'explode' when touched!

14

Otters are shy, playful animals that eat mostly fish.

Trout jump for insects.

Stonefly larvae

Caddisfly larvae make a case from tiny stones.

Willows are common waterside trees.

male catkins

Leaves are pale underneath

Stickleback

Minnow

Bullhead

See what you can catch in a jar of water – but let your prisoner go afterwards!

Dipper

Salmon return from the sea to spawn and will leap waterfalls on their journey upstream.

Look for them around October and November.

Butterbur leaves grow very big. Long ago they were used to wrap butter.

Look at the Osprey!

Many nature reserves have hides you can sit in.

Lakes and Ponds

Lakes, lochs and reservoirs can be huge and deep... then there are marshes, broads, ditches and ponds all waiting to be explored. Whatever you do: dipping with a net, paddling a canoe, sitting in a hide, or peering into a tiny garden pond, there's always something to see or hear... booming bitterns, spawning frogs, the splash of a hunting pike, tiny newts or a hovering dragonfly. You may even see a diving osprey, because although they nest in the north, they can turn up almost anywhere during their migration to and from Africa.

Herons are easily recognised. They spear fish and frogs with their huge beaks.

The **Great Diving Beetle** is a fierce predator, both as a nymph and as an adult.

Nymph

Adult

Common Toads have a dry, bumpy skin and crawl.

Common Frogs have wet, shiny skin and hop.

Newts can live in the tiniest garden pond.

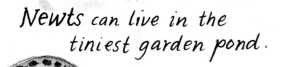

Palmate Newt

Frog-spawn

Toad-spawn

Stages of a Tadpole.

1 Hatchling

2 Back legs

3 Front legs

4. Froglet

'Toad-poles' are black.

16

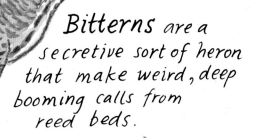

Bitterns *are a secretive sort of heron that make weird, deep booming calls from reed beds.*

Ospreys *are large birds that hover and make spectacular dives when fishing.*

Yellow   White

water Lily

Sedge Warblers *mimic other birds and add that to their busy song of clicks, trills and warbles.*

Purple Loosestrife

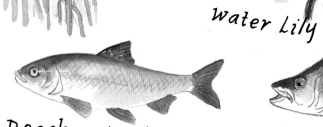

Roach *make rings on the surface as they rise for insects- and so do trout.*

Perch *splash the surface as they hunt, devouring small-fry.*

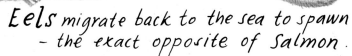

Eels *migrate back to the sea to spawn - the exact opposite of Salmon.*

Small fish breaking the surface is a sign of a hungry Pike.

Pike *can grow to1·8 metres (5 feet). They eat fish, ducklings and voles.*

17

WOODLAND

Beech Tree
Tall with muscular grey 'elephant skin' trunk

Leaves turn golden in autumn

Beech mast

Ash Tree
Long leaves give this tree a feathery look. Seeds hang like bunches of keys.

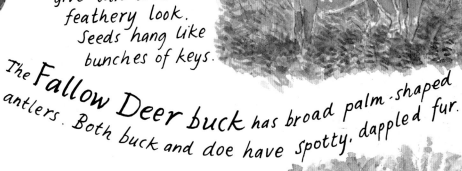

The **Fallow Deer buck** has broad palm-shaped antlers. Both buck and doe have spotty, dappled fur.

Elm Tree
Leaves are rough to the touch. Delicate winged seeds ripen in June.

The **Jay**'s noisy alarm call sounds like tearing paper.

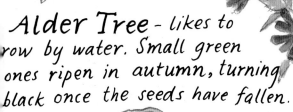

Alder Tree - likes to grow by water. Small green ones ripen in autumn, turning black once the seeds have fallen.

Red Campion
grows in woods and hedgerows.

Woodland
Trees absorb carbon and sulphur gas pollution and release oxygen for us to breathe. At all stages of their life cycle – from seed to rotten log – trees are essential for wildlife, providing food and shelter for thousands of different species. Woodlands change beautifully with every season: bare winter boughs, spring blossom, lush summer foliage, autumn leaves, fruits and seeds. Trees are rarely still and a storm blowing through a wood can sound as dramatic as a storm at sea.

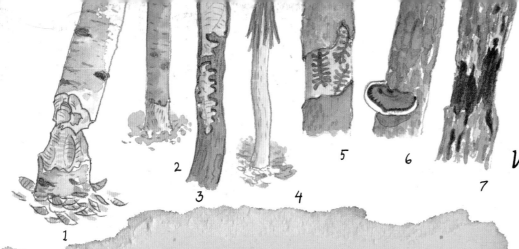

Once damaged, a decaying tree can be home to many living things, from fungi to insects.

What has damaged these trees?

1. Hungry beaver
2. Hungry hare
3 Hungry squirrel
4. Roebuck 'fraying' during rut
5. Beetle damage tracks under the bark
6. Growing fungus
7. Lightning burns from the inside

Broad-Leaved Trees

Even ornamental trees planted in a town car park will attract wildlife, but the more trees that grow together and the bigger the variety, the better. Exploring woods can feel mysterious: patches of light and shadow, the lazy hum of insects, the scent of wild garlic and the calls of unseen birds. Wood ants are a common sight foraging for food, and their nests, often built around a tree stump, can be over a metre (3 feet) high. In the autumn, broad-leaved trees shed their leaves to reduce the risk of winter storms blowing them over. Check out their beautiful colours and collect some leaves, nuts and seeds.

Fierce Ground Beetles hunt the woodland floor.

Jay Feather

Wood Ants defend their colony by biting and squirting a sort of acid.

Jays use ants to kill feather parasites.

Ant hills can be huge, with two queens and thousands of workers.

I'm talking to a Woodpecker!

Tap with a stick on a trunk to attract a curious woodpecker!

Silver Birch
Silver-white bark and golden spring catkins make this an easy tree to spot.

Lime Tree
Heart-shaped leaves with smooth surface and toothed edges

The **Willow Warbler** has a lovely summer song.

Listen for the laughing call and look for the bouncing flight of the Green Woodpecker.

The **Nuthatch** has a cheery, whistling call.

Rutting **Roebucks** 'attack' trees to clean away the velvety covering of their newly grown antlers. It's called **'fraying'.**

Maple Tree
Similar to the Sycamore but with rougher bark.

Oak Tree
Easily recognised by its leaves. An Oak may live for a thousand years.

The **Pied Flycatcher** dashes from its perch to catch insects.

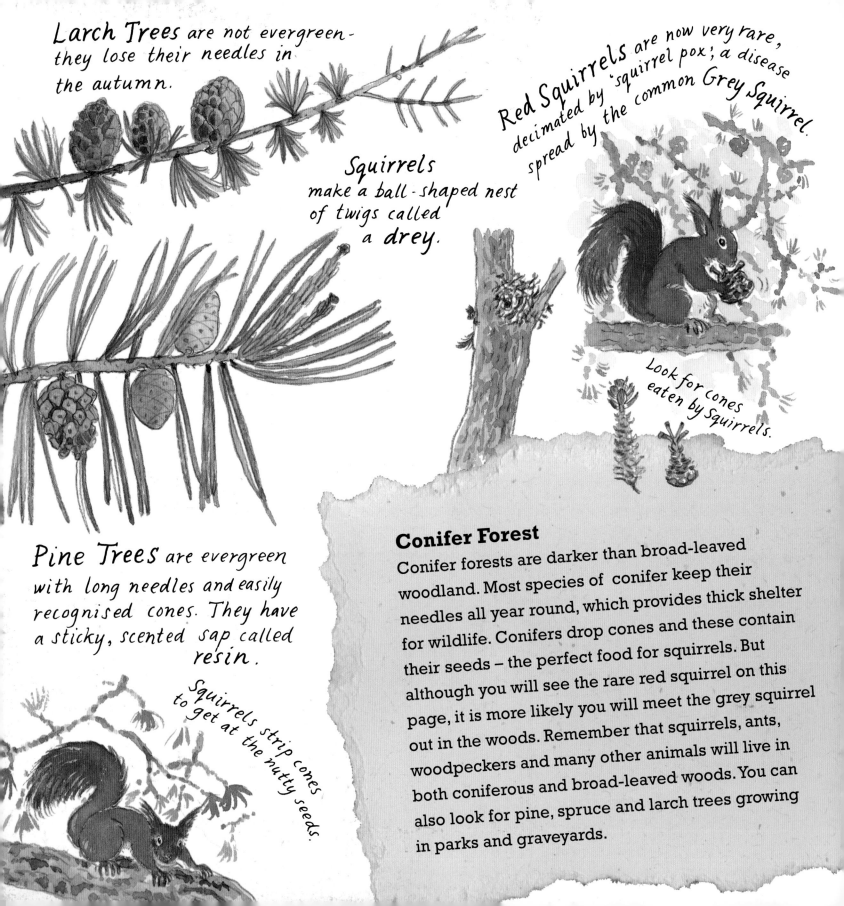

Larch Trees are not evergreen - they lose their needles in the autumn.

Red Squirrels are now very rare, decimated by 'squirrel pox', a disease spread by the common Grey Squirrel.

Squirrels make a ball-shaped nest of twigs called a **drey**.

Look for cones eaten by Squirrels.

Pine Trees are evergreen with long needles and easily recognised cones. They have a sticky, scented sap called **resin**.

Squirrels strip cones to get at the nutty seeds.

Conifer Forest

Conifer forests are darker than broad-leaved woodland. Most species of conifer keep their needles all year round, which provides thick shelter for wildlife. Conifers drop cones and these contain their seeds – the perfect food for squirrels. But although you will see the rare red squirrel on this page, it is more likely you will meet the grey squirrel out in the woods. Remember that squirrels, ants, woodpeckers and many other animals will live in both coniferous and broad-leaved woods. You can also look for pine, spruce and larch trees growing in parks and graveyards.

The *Great Spotted Woodpecker* has a bouncing flight. Listen for the hammering sound as it taps on old trees. Woodpeckers love to feed on grubs that tunnel in rotten wood.

Woodpeckers chisel nest-holes in old tree trunks. The chicks can be quite noisy.

Spruce is also known as the 'Christmas Tree'.

Look for the dashing *Sparrowhawk* as it hunts through wood, garden and hedgerow.

Make a cast of tracks.

Carry strips of card, paper clips, plaster of Paris, a bottle of water and a mixing jug in a rucksack.

① Find a good clear track in mud or sand. Clear away twigs or leaves.

② Bend a strip of card into a circle big enough to fit the footprint and fix it with a paper clip.

③ Using a stick, mix plaster of Paris and clean water until it is the texture of thick yoghurt.

④ Pour into the cardboard mould. Leave for 20 minutes.

⑤ Take it home and label it.

Wait for it to set hard.

Name and date your plaster cast track.

How to check if a sett is occupied
Lightly place two sticks across the entrance. Are they pushed away next time you visit.?

Five-toed, bear-like tracks of a badger

Badger-watching

Always stand downwind from the sett and don't make any sounds, because although badgers have poor eyesight they have good senses of smell and hearing.

If you are lucky you might see badger cubs playing rough and tumble.

Woods at Night

It's not so easy, or safe, to visit a wood at night without an adult. But many regional wildlife groups run organised trips to watch animals like badgers and bats. Try contacting your local natural history group or Wildlife Trust (see p.49) and browse the internet to find out what's on near you. Your first badger-watching adventure is something you will never forget. I still remember mine, and that happened forty years ago.

"Then nightly sings the staring owl..."
William Shakespeare

Tawny Owls can often be heard at night calling to each other. You can get them to reply if you learn to hoot like this.

Listen for the 'roding' display flight of the male **Woodcock**. He patrols the boundary of his territory at dusk, making grunts and whistles.

Tawny Owls call to each other: "Keewick!" "Hoo-hoo!" They like woodland but can live in many habitats.

Male **Nightjars** have white flashes on their wings. Listen for their unearthly two-tone churring call after sunset and the whip-like crack of their wing-clap display.

Nightjars are nocturnal insect-eaters that live on the edges of woods, young plantations and heathland.

Long-Eared Owls prefer conifer forests and are very shy.

Owl pellets

Owls feed on small mammals, birds, worms and insects. They cannot digest hard bones, so they cough them up wrapped in fur and feathers. This is called a **pellet**.

Beetle wing case

Field Vole

If you find a pellet, take it home and soak it in warm water for 5 minutes. Poke it apart to see what's inside. Then wash your hands!

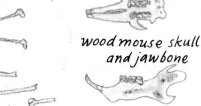

Owl pellet. Look for them under fence posts and roosting sites.

Bird beaks

Bird bones

wood mouse skull and jawbone

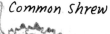

Common Shrew

FIELD AND HEDGEROW

Moles live underground, eating the worms that fall into their tunnel traps. Molehills are where they push up the soil.

Field and Hedgerow

Hedges can be hundreds of years old. Traditionally planted as windbreaks to give shelter to crops and livestock, hedges are an essential but declining habitat for wildlife to nest in, burrow under and feed from. Many animals, including deer, rabbits, hares and voles feed in fields, and in autumn flocks of birds gather to gorge on the juicy berry crops produced by hedgerow plants. Watch for the ghostly barn owl, the hovering kestrel and the hedge-dodging sparrowhawk keeping the small birds and mammals under control.

Roe Deer often venture out from cover to feed in fields.

Hawthorn is the commonest hedgerow plant.

May blossom

Fieldfare   Redwing

Kestrel
A common bird of prey that hovers as it hunts for mice and voles.

Elder

female
male

Pheasants

Huge winter flocks of Fieldfares and Redwings gather to feed in fields and on the many juicy hedgerow berries.

Blackberry or Bramble

Blackthorn or Sloe

Holly

Dog Rose, also known as Wild Rose and Briar

rosehip

27

Stoats and Weasels are playful hunters that can follow their prey down holes and into dry-stone walls.

Tracks

Stoats are chestnut brown with a bushy, black-tipped tail.

Dropping

In cold winters they change colour. A white stoat is called an Ermine.

Weasels are much smaller with a stumpy tail.

Along the Hedge

Look for animal pathways through fields and hedges. Small burrows may belong to rabbits, mice, voles or rats. Larger holes could belong to badgers or foxes (a fox den will smell musky). Many hedge plants were originally chosen because of their thorns, so be careful. Have a close look and you might find strands of animal fur snagged in their prickles: gingery fox hair, grey badger bristles and brown rabbit fluff. Sticky-tape the fur samples into your notebook, and learn the grass-squeal. It really works! I once had a weasel sit on my boot for a better look at me.

male - dog fox
female - vixen

FOXES can be found in many habitats. They will eat just about anything from meat to berries. They are mostly nocturnal but often hunt before sunset.

FOXES mark their territory with a musky scent that smells rather like fried garlic and tomatoes!

Harebell

Thistle

Cow Parsley

Hazel nut eaten by a Vole

Shrews eat insects and worms.

Field Vole

Wood Mouse

Hazel nut eaten by a Mouse.

Common Grasses

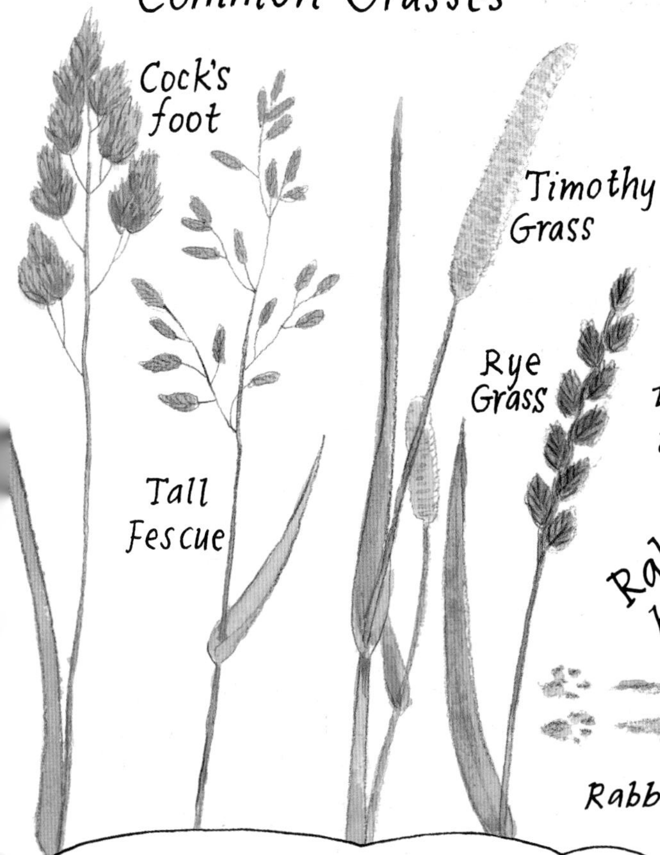

Cock's foot

Timothy Grass

Rye Grass

Tall Fescue

Rabbits live in burrows. A rabbit warren has many entrances, and is scattered with small round droppings.

Rabbits hop and are smaller than hares.

Rabbit tracks

Yellowhammers seem to sing: "a-little-bit o'bread and no cheeeese.'"

'Wee, sleekit, cowrin, tim'rous beastie,' - Robert Burns

It's important to stretch the grass tight and blow between your thumbs.

Squeal like an injured rabbit by blowing through a blade of grass. It might attract a stoat or even a fox.

The spiky **Gorse** flowers all year round.

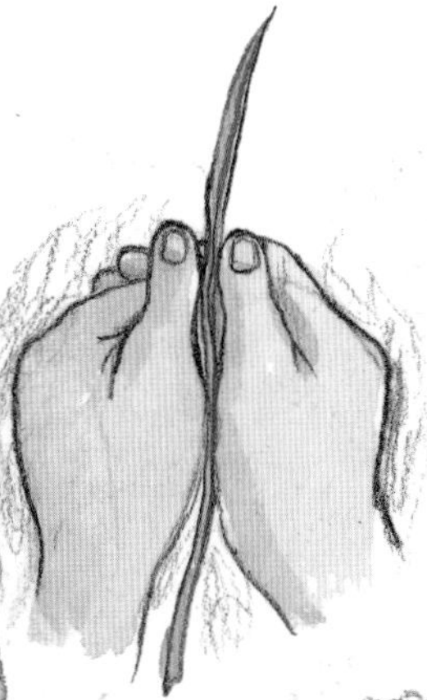

Hares are bigger than rabbits and live above ground. They can run like the wind!

Hare track

29

This reminds me of Ted Hughes' poem, 'Coming down through Somerset'.

The Red Kite is easily recognised by its forked tail.

male

Kestrels hunt the grass verges for small mammals.

female

Buzzards often sit by the road-side looking for Road-kill...

Toads are trapped by high kerbs when crossing en-masse to spring breeding ponds.

Rolling up into a prickly ball doesn't protect the Hedgehog.

Hares can outrun predators such as foxes... but not cars.

Road Journeys

A glimpse of a hovering kestrel can brighten any road or rail journey, and by night a badger or fox glimpsed in the car headlights is a thrill. Roadside verges and hedgerows are important habitats and provide 'wildlife corridors' that connect pockets of green space; but they are also dangerous places. More gamekeepers' pheasants are killed by traffic than by foxes! 'Road-kill' often becomes food for something else such as a scavenging fox or buzzard. But if nothing eats that sad bundle of fur or feathers then fly maggots and beetle grubs will soon begin their life-cycle. Nothing is wasted in the natural world.

Sexton Beetles: part of the 'clean-up squad'

Tracks

Roe Deer

Cat

Badger

Red Deer

Print quality can vary according to how wet the mud or sand is.

Gull

A typical wader track

Oystercatcher probing the mud

Swan

Egg Shells

Song Thrush's egg...

...eaten by a Weasel

...hatched

Blackbird

Crow

Coot's egg eaten by a Crow

Footpaths

Pathways are not just made by humans. The network of trails from a badger sett, leading up-hill and down-dale, can be hundreds of years old. Many animals use our footpaths too, so keep your ears and eyes open for tracks, prey remains, droppings, calls, songs – and, if you're quiet, some of the animals that made them. Like any nature adventure, try to keep the breeze in your face so animals don't get your scent and if you see something, freeze! Creep closer only when an animal's attention is elsewhere – a feeding deer or a diving otter for example.

If you find a dead bird with a ring on its leg...

...send the details to the address on the ring.

Droppings

Hedgehog

Badger

Badgers dig holes to use as a toilet. This dropping contains beetles and grain.

Fox

Look for the twisted, pointy end. Colour and texture depend on what has been eaten.

Red Deer

Rabbits use droppings to mark their territory.

Mouse

Vole

Prey Remains

A bird of prey leaves 'v'-shaped beak marks in a breast-bone as it feeds.

Green Woodpecker dropping containing ant fragments packed inside an ash-grey 'wrapping'

Rabbit skulls are a common find.

31

WILD COUNTRY

A moor is a good place to see birds of prey, including owls.

Elbow patches

Flies like a ghost!

Barn Owl
Heart-shaped facial disc, pale body and dark eyes.

Little Owl
Small with 'angry' yellow eyes, often seen in daylight.

This Peregrine Falcon has caught a Lapwing

A Peregrine Falcon 'stoops' on its prey.

Short-Eared Owl
Has a fierce goblin's glare and often hunts by day - especially in the winter.

Scattered feathers are a sign a predator has made a kill. If the feathers have been chewed, it was a mammal, but if plucked - it was a bird of prey!

Lapwing

Collect and keep any clean skulls or feathers. What else can you find?

Curlew Skull

Wild country!
Moorland, mountain, rough grassland, peat bog and heath. Lonely places where the wind blows freely through tough plants such as heather, rush, bracken, bilberry and bog cotton. Owls and other birds of prey love wild country and these habitats are perfect for all sorts of nature adventures. Spring and summer are probably the best time to get your boots on and go exploring.

Wood Pigeon

Grouse

Short-Eared Owl

Lapwing

Lapwing

chewed

plucked

Snipe

moulted

Sometimes feathers fall out naturally due to moulting.

33

Listen for the liquid bubbling call of the **curlew**.

curved beak

Skylarks sing their hearts out as they climb higher and higher into the sky.

Chirrup Chirrup...

'Bzzzzzz'

Grasshopper

Reminds me of *The Lark Ascending* by Vaughan Williams.

Lapwings tumble in the sky, making a throaty 'pee-wit' cry.

Snipe climb steeply, then dive making the air hum through their tail feathers. This display is called 'drumming.'

Golden Plovers have a lonely whistling call.

Carrion and **Hooded Crows** croak.

What can you hear? Sheep bleat, grasshoppers chirrup, bees buzz, and falcons go...

keee keee kee!
keee kee!
kee! kee!
keee!

Buzzards circle and make a mewing call - 'Weeooww weeooww.'

Ravens are bigger with a kite-shaped tail. They make lots of sounds, including a deep 'Krup Krup'.

Wheatear

Tchack! Tchack!

Red Grouse seem to grumble at you from the heather. 'Go-back-go-back-go-back!'

Red Deer live in wildplaces such as moors and mountains. You might even find an antler.

Look out for the huge Golden Eagle, only seen in very remote areas. It feeds mostly on carrion, rabbits and hares.

'There is a spot,
'mid barren hills,
Where winter howls...'
Emily Brontë

Sit with your back to a wall and listen.....
Can you hear the wind whispering?

Up on the Moor

What sort of animals you see and hear on a moor will depend on where you are and what time of year it is. I grew up on the moors, and as a boy was lucky enough to see and hear all the animals I have drawn on this page and others such as foxes and weasels. Remember, when you step into wild country – or on any other nature adventure – use your eyes, nose and ears and soak up that delicious 'wild' atmosphere.

Common Cotton Grass or 'Bog Cotton'

Soft Rush

Heather

Honey Bee

Bilberry

Grass Snakes like to live near water. They eat frogs, mice and voles.

Adders use their venomous bite to stun prey such as mice and voles.

THE SEASHORE

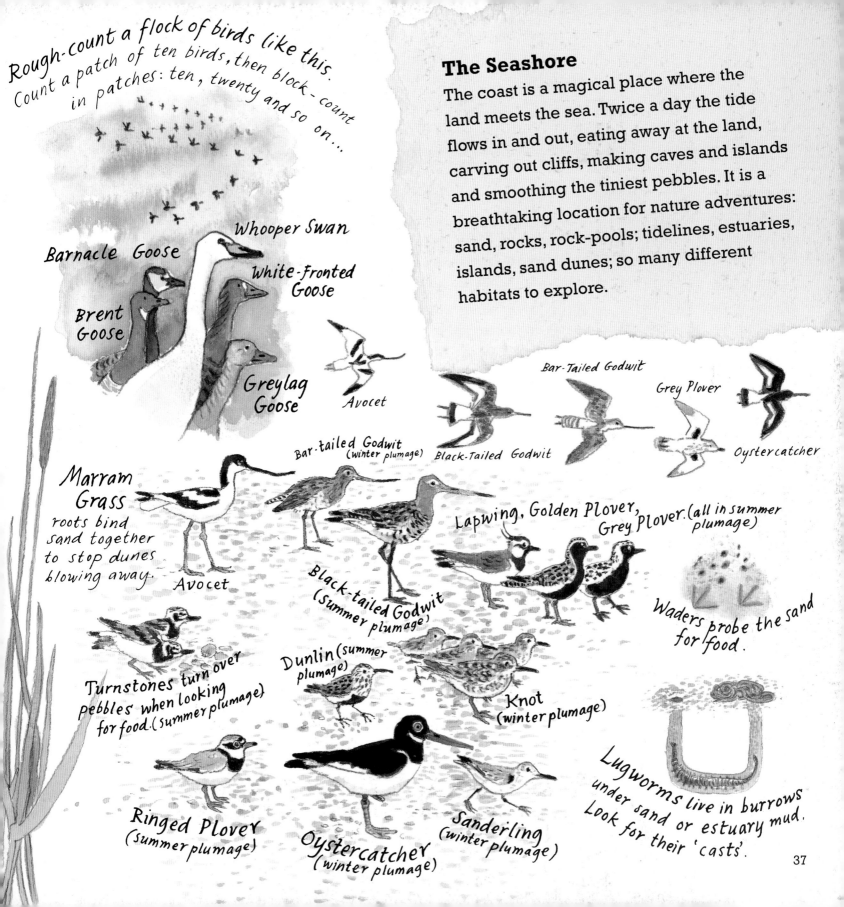

Rough-count a flock of birds like this.
Count a patch of ten birds, then block-count in patches: ten, twenty and so on...

The Seashore

The coast is a magical place where the land meets the sea. Twice a day the tide flows in and out, eating away at the land, carving out cliffs, making caves and islands and smoothing the tiniest pebbles. It is a breathtaking location for nature adventures: sand, rocks, rock-pools; tidelines, estuaries, islands, sand dunes; so many different habitats to explore.

Barnacle Goose

Whooper Swan

White-Fronted Goose

Brent Goose

Greylag Goose

Avocet

Bar-Tailed Godwit

Grey Plover

Black-Tailed Godwit

Oystercatcher

Bar-tailed Godwit (winter plumage)

Marram Grass roots bind sand together to stop dunes blowing away.

Avocet

Black-tailed Godwit (summer plumage)

Lapwing, Golden Plover, Grey Plover. (all in summer plumage)

Waders probe the sand for food.

Turnstones turn over pebbles when looking for food. (summer plumage)

Dunlin (summer plumage)

Knot (winter plumage)

Ringed Plover (summer plumage)

Oystercatcher (winter plumage)

Sanderling (winter plumage)

Lugworms live in burrows under sand or estuary mud. Look for their 'casts'.

37

Grey Seals and Common Seals come close inshore.

Sometimes they will haul-out on rocks or quiet beaches... Listen for their wailing song carried on the breeze.

Winter Diving Birds

Long-Tailed Duck

Smew

Black-Necked Grebe

Guillemot

Razorbill

Little Auk

Cormorant – white face and thigh patches in summer

A Shag is greener and has a yellow 'grin'.

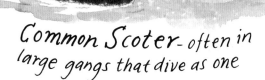

Common Scoter – often in large gangs that dive as one

Goosander   **Merganser**

female

male

male

female

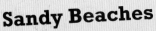

Sandy Beaches

Battered by storms, baked by sun and salty winds; washed twice a day by the tide, beaches are a home for many creatures. At high tide fish swim over the sand, crabs and shellfish come out to feed and seals and seabirds hunt them for food. Then at low tide it's all change! Waders probe the sand for worms and sandhoppers and alongside them, other animals find food in the flotsam left on the tideline. It's amazing what the sea washes ashore – beachcombing can turn up almost anything.

Shelducks like to nest in old rabbit holes in sand dunes.

Flatfish like **Plaice** love sandy beaches

Terns are noisy birds with forked tails that dive for fish.

"Tyu-hu-tyu-hu..."

Common Tern

Sandwich Tern

Cuttlefish bone

Redshank give a noisy alarm call.

The **Weaver Fish** hides in the sand on some beaches. Its spines can give an agonizing sting to bare feet!

'Lonely the seabird lies at her rest, Blown like a dawn-blenched parcel of spray...' That's by W.B. Yeats.

Razor Shell

Top Shell

This **Mermaid's Purse** is the egg-case of a **Dogfish**.

Collecting shells and other things washed up by the tide is one of the pleasures of a visit to the seaside.

This **Oystercatcher's** beak has faded over time.

Scallop

Cockle

Wendletrap

Jellyfish are often stranded by the tide.

Sea Urchin skeleton or 'test'

39

whelk

Barnacle

Limpet

Dog Whelks prey on other molluscs by boring a hole through their shells.

Winkle

Look out for the evidence of broken shells...

Oystercatchers open shellfish with their beaks.

Mussel

Hermit Crabs take over empty shells.

'To see a world in a grain of sand
And heaven in a wild flower.'
William Blake

Shore Crabs can be found under rocks at low tide – and **Starfish** too... But always replace rocks as you found them.

Sand Hoppers live in the sand and also in piles of rotting seaweed.

Rockpool Wildlife

closed   open

Seaweed is like an underwater forest.

Shanny

Beadlet Anemone

Butterfish

Common Goby

Bladderwrack

Kelp

Gannets dive for fish from a great height like arrows!

Great Black-Backed Gulls are big, aggressive predators.

Common Gull

Kittiwakes seem to repeat their own name "Kittiwake-Kittiwake!"

Gannets look very white, with black wingtips.

Fulmars are related to Albatrosses.

Guillemot

Razorbill

Puffin

Thrift or *Sea Pink* grows well on cliffs.

Grey Seals can be attracted by singing. Try warbling like an opera singer! They are nosy and will often come closer!

Grey Seal pups are born around November.

male   female

Eider Ducks. Males make an excited "ooooh!" sound when displaying to the females.

Rocks

Rocky shores are hard and angular. Carved out by centuries of wind and waves they often jut far out into deep water. Cliffs and islands are used as nesting sites by many sorts of seabird. But be careful - rocks can be slippery and cliffs can crumble. Peer into a rock-pool at low tide - it's a world in miniature. Look under loose rocks to find crabs, starfish and other shore-life, but always put the rocks back as you found them and leave limpets and other shore-life in peace. Keep an eye on the tide so you never get trapped.

THROUGH THE SEASONS

scar

"Cuckoo, Cuckoo!"
Cuckoos lay their eggs in other birds' nests.

male cuckoo

Fox Cubs are born in Spring and their dens become littered with prey remains.

Swifts chase each other, screaming loudly.

Coltsfoot

Primrose

Cowslip

Horse Chestnuts burst into leaf. Look out for the horse-shoe shaped scar from last year's leaf stalk.

Toastie Recipe:
A handful of wild garlic (only the leaves) Grilled on toast with grated cheese.

Spring

When spring arrives it feels as if nature has suddenly woken up and is late for school. Everything seems in a rush. Early flowers, leaf buds and blossoms burst open and many birds begin the dawn chorus. Can you identify which birds are singing? Watch for nest-building birds in parks and gardens; but don't disturb them. Look for frog-spawn and listen for the first fat bumblebee queens revving about like noisy speedway motorbikers.

Yellow Underwing Moths *fly by night.*

Summer

Summer's warmth is good for insects: butterflies and moths, grasshoppers and crickets, bees and wasps, houseflies and bluebottles. After dusk on summer nights try attracting moths to a white sheet by torchlight. What else is out there? Bats, toads, snails and slugs - perhaps even a hedgehog. Don't forget your notebook.

House Martins *are dark blue and white birds with short 'V'shaped tails.*

Swallows *are more elegant with long tail-streamers.*

'The fat cock Thrush To his nest has gone;'

'And the dew shines bright In the rising Moon;' Walter De la Mare

Shine a torch on a sheet and note what insects land in the pool of light.

Honeysuckle

Foxglove

Hummingbird Hawk-Moths *fly by day.*

Woodland Flowers

Lily of the Valley

Wild Garlic

Bluebell

Garden Tiger Moth

Wood Anemone

43

Flocks of *Fieldfares* and *Redwings* arrive to spend winter with us.

"*Season of mists and mellow fruitfulness!*" wrote John Keats.

Autumn

Autumn is when many trees lose their leaves and drop nuts and seeds. Forage for conkers, beech mast and acorns once the autumn winds begin to blow. Autumn is also a good time to spot fungi, but don't touch because many can be poisonous. Look and listen for flocks of winter visitors such as gaggles of geese and 'chack-chacking' fieldfares, and on still nights go outdoors and listen for the thin 'seeep-seeep' call of redwings.

Fungi grow well in early autumn.

Leaf litter is home and food for many mini-beasts.

Fly Agaric is very poisonous.

The *Stinkhorn's* smell of rotten meat attracts flies that help disperse its spores.

Harvestman

Worms drag leaves underground for food.

Dormice begin to hibernate by late autumn.

44

Winter

Winter snow and ice can cover and freeze the drinking water birds and mammals rely on, so remember to put out fresh water as well as food. Look out for the acrobatic flight patterns of starling and wader flocks, designed to confuse birds of prey. By late winter the fat buds, bulging on many tree branches, are a sure sign that spring is just around the corner.

Winter visitors such as **Waxwings** can be seen feeding on berries even in the town.

Listen for their 'worried' twittering call.

Winter Twigs

Horse Chestnut

Ash

Beech

Hazel

Silver Birch

Lime

Sycamore

Oak

Hawthorn

Look for tracks in **Snow...**

Fox

Pet dog

In the winter, Starlings roost together in huge, noisy, acrobatic flocks. They like the warmth of towns and shopping centres.

'Yes, of course it hurts when buds are bursting. Why else should springtime hesitate?'
Karin Boye

Rowan

The frosted web of an Orb Spider

GLOSSARY

Beachcombing – the activity of searching for interesting objects washed up on the tide.

Carbon and sulphur gas – these gases are major causes of air pollution.

Cemetery – a burial ground often planted with trees. Some cemeteries like Highgate Cemetery in London can be very old, huge and overgrown. They make a sheltered place for wildlife to live.

Carnivore – meat-eater, a stoat for example.

Dawn chorus – the spring song of birds that begins before daylight.

Diurnal – active in the day.

Drumming – A snipe's display flight. The bleating sound as air rushes through the tail feathers.

Food chain – for example snail, eaten by thrush, eaten by sparrowhawk.

Insectivore – insect-eater, a hedgehog for example.

Life cycle – the stages in an animal's life from birth to death.

Metamorphosis – a process by which insects and some other sorts of animals can completely change their body shape, often while inside a pupa – but the changes can also happen more gradually over weeks or years, such as tadpole to frog or nymph to dragonfly.

Mimic – to copy another's behaviour. Some birds copy other birds' songs for example.

Mollusc – an animal without a backbone, protected by a shell, such as a snail or a shellfish.

Nature reserves – areas of land set aside for wildlife.

Nocturnal – active at night.

Nymph – the young of many water insects such as dragonflies (but also land insects such as grasshoppers). Nymphs undergo gradual metamorphosis and this can take up to four years or longer in a dragonfly. They reach their adult stage without becoming a pupa.

Omnivore – eats both meat and plants, a badger for example.

Parasite – an animal that lives off another, for example a louse or a tick.

Pellet – the indigestible parts of a bird's food, coughed up. Many birds cough up pellets, from rooks and gulls to birds of prey.

Pesticides – garden poisons sometime used to kill weeds and pests. They can be harmful to other wildlife and pass into the food chain.

Plucked – when a bird is de-feathered before being eaten.

Predator – an animal that preys on others.

Pupa – the stage of transformation in the life cycle common to many insects that undergo complete metamorphosis through four life stages: egg, larva, pupa and adult.

Rings – some birds carry numbered leg rings or tags. Send the number and details of where you found it to the address on the ring or tag.

Road-kill – animals run-over by traffic.

Reservoir – an artificial lake used as a water supply, and a good place to see water birds, especially in winter.

Species diversity – the variety of living things in a given area.

Squirrel Pox – a disease passed on to red squirrels from greys.

Spawn – the eggs of fish and amphibians.

Spore – microscopic structures produced by fungi and some other living things. Spores are dispersed by the wind or stick to insects' feet to grow into new individuals.

Stoop – the power-dive of a peregrine falcon as it swoops on its prey. It can reach almost 200 miles per hour.

Test – the empty shell of a sea urchin. The one illustrated is a heart urchin.

Tracks – footprints or other nature signs left by wildlife.

Urban – a word referring to built-up areas like towns.

Vegetarian – eats only plants, a deer for example.

Safety Note
- Nature adventures can be thrilling and inspiring – but you must always be sensible, use your common sense and stay safe.
- Never go off without telling a trusted grown-up where you are going and never trust a stranger.
- Never climb cliffs, go too close to deep water or take risks with the tides.
- Keep away from busy roads.
- Follow the country code by closing gates and not lighting fires.
- Don't drop litter and don't disturb wildlife.
- Remember to wash your hands after handling any nature finds.

LIST OF POEMS AND MUSIC

male

Stonechats make a sound like pebbles knocking together.

male

Reed Buntings like wild country.

Privet Hawk Moth Caterpillar

ACKNOWLEDGEMENTS:

Daddy Fell into the Pond – lines reprinted by kind permission of the Society of Authors, as the literary representatives of the Estate of Alfred Noyes

Berries, Old Shellover – lines reprinted by kind permission of the Literary Trustees of Walter de la Mare and the Society of Authors as their representative

Sea Fever – lines reprinted by kind permission of The Society of Authors, as the literary representatives of the Estate of John Masefield

Of Course It Hurts – original Swedish copyright © 1935 Ulf Boye, English translation copyright © 2011 Brita Granström

Bush Cricket

THE WILDLIFE TRUSTS

The Wildlife Trusts are all about local wildlife conservation. There are 47 individual Wildlife Trusts covering every part of the UK which means there will be one looking after wildlife and wild places near you, wherever you live. We have more than 2,250 nature reserves, looking after all the wildlife habitats found in the UK, including wildflower meadows, ancient woodlands, lakes, moors, hills, heaths, estuaries and beaches. They are fantastic places for you and your family to explore and enjoy local wildlife. Some of the largest reserves have visitor centres and every year thousands of schools visit us to discover more about their local wildlife.

Wildlife Watch is the junior branch of The Wildlife Trusts and the UK's leading environmental action club for kids. If you care about nature and the environment and want to explore your local wildlife – this is the club for you! Wildlife Watch members receive loads of exciting wildlife goodies throughout the year, including a starter pack and four issues of Wildlife Watch magazine a year. This is packed full of amazing pictures, puzzles and competitions, and a fantastic free wildlife poster comes with each issue. Plus there's also the chance to get access to local activities and events. We also have a really wild website (*www.wildlifewatch.org.uk*) and a free monthly e-newsletter packed full of wild ideas and nature-spotting tips. And the best thing about being a member is that by joining Wildlife Watch you'll be helping your local Wildlife Trust to care for the wildlife where you live! Isn't that great?

For more information on membership go to:
www.wildlifewatch.org.uk/membership
For more information on The Wildlife Trusts go to:
www.wildlifetrusts.org

Protecting Wildlife for the Future